Glimpses of Guernsey

Interesting stories and traditions of the Bailiwick

John Manning

© John Manning

All rights reserved. No part of this publication may be reproduced, stored in a retrieval system, or transmitted, in any form or by any means, electronic, mechanical, photocopying, recording or otherwise, without the prior permission of John Manning.

Published 1995.

Made and printed in Great Britain by
The Guernsey Press Co. Ltd, Guernsey, Channel Islands.

ISBN 0 902550 54 3

CONTENTS

Birth of the Islands	5
The Bridge	7
Chapel of St Apolline	9
Special Delivery	12
Les Casquettes	16
Milk-o-Punch Sunday	19
The Master of Sempill	21
A Second Posting	23
La Gran' Mère du Cimétière	25
Empire Electric Theatre	27
The Picquet House	29
Alderney Wins Muratti	31
First British Post Boxes	34
The Little Chapel	37
Victoria Tower	39
Silver Mines on Sark	42
Bungalow Hotel	45
Sir Peter Osborne and Castle Cornet	48
Beaucette Marina	51
St George's Hall	55
The Channel Islands' First Airport	57
C.I. Occupation Stamps	60

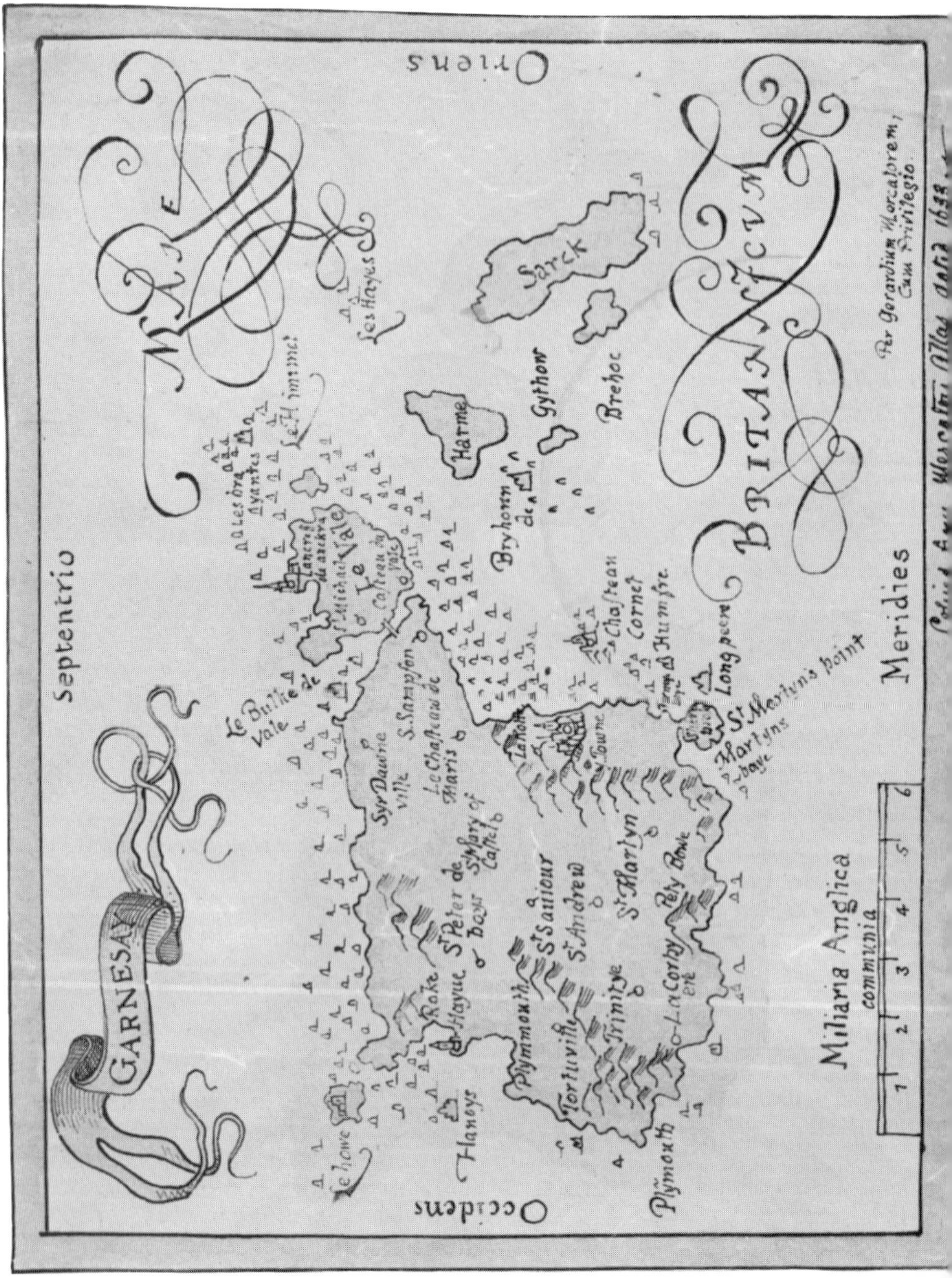
GARNESAY
Septentrio
Oriens
Occidens
Meridies
MARE BRITANNICUM
Sarck
Harme
Brehoc
Gythow
Les Hayes
Le Vale
Le Bulke de Vale
S. Sampson
St Peter de Port
St Saulour
St Andrew
St Martyn
Plymmouth
Tortuville
Trinitye
Longpere
Le Chasteau de Maris
St Martyns point
Hanoys
Le Howe
Miliaria Anglica communia
1
2
3
4
5
6
Per Gerardum Mercatorem,
Cum Privilegio.

BIRTH OF THE ISLANDS

BEFORE the Great Ice Age, Europe was one large continent with a mighty river flowing where the English Channel now divides Britain and France. Numerous tributaries branched off the main river, flowing both north and south, until eventually the water reached the Atlantic Ocean. At this period of time the Channel Islands did not exist. They would have been small, high plateaux of land standing out on the grassy plains of the huge continent. As the ice melted great areas of land were swallowed up by the waters and the river became larger until a vast channel was cut between England and France. Only the few high plateaux of rock remained and these formed the Channel Islands. The speed of this process has been calculated at 18 inches each century. Guernsey was believed to be the first island to appear, 14,000 years ago, followed by Alderney and Sark which separated from Guernsey 11,000 years ago, finally Jersey, Herm and Jethou became islands only 4,500 years ago.

Over the centuries these islands have been inhabited and over-run by different races of people, therefore the names of the islands changed periodically. Some of these names have been recorded, others simply disappeared with the passing of time.

The first written recording of the islands can be found in the Antonine Itinerary which appeared about AD284. During this period the islands were part of the province of Lugdunensis after the division of Gaul by the Emperor Augustus, who was the successor to Julius Caesar. The Romans were constantly crossing the Channel and part of the Itinerary listed the islands, in order to aid the officials on what must have been a long hazardous journey. The names given in the Itinerary were; Riduna; Lesia; Sarmia; Andium and Caesarea.

Riduna was Alderney and remains of this old name can still be found on our northern island. The Romans would have named the largest land mass after Caesar and at this period of time this would have been the Minquiers. Sarmia was Sark leaving Lesia for Guernsey and Andium for Jersey.

The Romans were later conquered by the Franks and in AD511 the islands became part of the Kingdom of Neustria. This would have been the first time we were under the rule of the Germans.

When St. Sampson came to the islands in AD530 seeking to bring Christianity to these small outposts of the province, Guernsey was still Lesia with Jersey now called Angia. It was around this period that Christian Britons, living in Devon and Cornwall, then known as South Wales, were informed that a large part of the province of Armorica in northern France was deserted and so they came in their thousands to settle and cultivate the land. Hence the name of Brittany and the population known as Bretons.

In AD800 Abbot Gervold from St Wandrille was sent on a mission and landed on the island of Angia which was ruled by a chief named Andwareth. The letters AN was the Celtic name for large and Jersey was the largest of the populated islands. Also the Saxon word for surrounded by water was Augia. Therefore an amalgamation of the two would mean the large area surrounded by water.

It is with the arrival of the Vikings in the 9th century that the first mention of our modern names can be found. EY was Norse for island and OU for an islet, whilst the Frisian word for grass is Gers. Add EY for island and we can understand how in numerous old books we find mention of Gersui - Gersey and Gerseye. This would have eventually led to Jersey - the grassy island.

There is a suggestion Guernsey was named after a Viking chief called Guernin. With EY on the end it could be the beginning of the name Guernsey - the island of Guernin.

Another school of thought is the islands were named after two rivers in France. Jersey is close to Carteret which was at the mouth of the river Ger or Gerfleur, whilst Guernsey is opposite the exit of the river Le Guer. In both cases the ending EY would ressemble our modern names.

The OU for islet would account for our numerous small islands such as Jethou, Lihou, Brecqhou and Burhou.

In the Patent Rolls of 1456 more variations of the islands names can be found and the relevant passage from the Rolls is as follows;

Island	Roman	Dark Ages	Middle Ages
Alderney	Riduna	Adreni	Arenon
Guernsey	Lesia	Lesia	Garnereia
Sark	Sarmia	Sargia	Sercque
Jersey	Andium	Angia	Jarzay
Herm	Barsa	Rima	Erm-Erme
Minquiers	Caesarea	Men-ker	Minquiers

It is interesting to record that the first mention of Sarnia for Guernsey is in Camden's *Britannia* in 1586 although from the above Rolls it does look as if the original Sarnia or Sarmia was Sark.

There are numerous schools of thought as to the origin of the modern names of our islands with no one school being able to provide conclusive proof that their theory is the correct version. I have tried to piece together the common ground of these different ideas and now leave it to the readers to form their own conclusions on the subject.

THE BRIDGE

UNTIL 1806 Guernsey was a divided island, a narrow channel, ranging in width from 50 yards to half a mile, split the main area of land from a small section in the north-east known as Clos du Valle. This channel, the Braye du Valle, stretched from St Sampson's to Grand Havre and was a great source of income to many islanders who extracted salt from the sea around Grand Fort and the area still known as Saltpans.

Twice daily, at high tide, the sea filled the Braye to a depth of 20 feet whilst at low tide the area became an uncrossable valley of mud. Many pirate ships made St Sampson's their first call after sailing from England to enable them to stock up with salt before marauding the seas for plunder.

Eventually, two means of crossing the Braye were constructed. At L'Islet a stone causeway called Pont St Michel enabled people to cross at low tide whilst a ferry operated when sufficient water filled the Braye. Many of the congregation of Vale Church had to use this ferry service to go to Sunday prayers.

Only small fishing boats were able to use the Braye due to the depth of water, therefore larger vessels anchored on the sands near St Sampson's. It was from here that the stone from the quarries in the north of Guernsey was exported.

The stone industry began in 1760, making the natural harbour of St Sampson's an extremely busy seaport. Therefore it was essential to have a good crossing over the Braye and a stone bridge, complete with sluice gate, was constructed. The bridge, known as Le Grand Pont, was large enough to accomodate both pedestrians and horse and carriages. The many labourers who loaded the ships at low tide must have been thankful to have a dry safe crossing over the Braye.

After the unsuccessful attempt by the French to capture Jersey in 1781, there was a strong feeling the next attack could be directed at Guernsey. The Clos du Valle, isolated from the main part of the island by the Braye, was thought to be the ideal base camp for such an attack.

In 1806, Sir John Doyle, Lieut-Governor of Guernsey, enlisted the financial backing of the British Government to reclaim the land of Braye du Valle.

He was placed in charge of a large force of English and Militia soldiers plus a strong naval attachment and proceeded to construct two dams, one at each end of the Braye.

The channel was then filled in and a total of 732 vergees and 6 perches of land were reclaimed from the sea. Compensation had to be paid, mainly to the owners of the Saltpans, and this amounted to £3,250, although this was also reclaimed by selling the land for £5,000.

One clause in the deed of sale made the owners of the new land responsible for the upkeep of the bridge. This continued until 1872 when a final payment of £50 relieved the landowners of this task. Sir John Doyle used part of the £5,000 to build new military roads enabling his troops to move quickly to all parts of the island.

During the 1880's the natural harbour of St Sampson's was enlarged with numerous piers and jetties. Some lasted the test of time whilst others fell into ruin. A new industry blossomed with the opening of Stonelake and Rankilor shipbuilding yards and many fine vessels received their first taste of water at St Sampson's. Houses were required for the workers and fishermen and Mr Stonelake used his workforce during slack periods to build houses around the bridge and many of these still exist in their original form.

Many forms of transport have been used between St Peter Port and St Sampson's. From the horse and cart to electric trams and steam driven trains. All these modes of commuting must have been far more leisurely and picturesque than the constant stream of traffic we find today.

Nevertheless, St Sampson's has retained a certain amount of old world charm. Coupled with relatively easy parking this has meant a continual growth in the area, a total contrast to the days when the Bridge simply meant the only access at all states of the tide across the Braye du Valle.

CHAPEL OF ST APOLLINE

DURING the reign of the Roman Emperor Decius, there was a purge throughout Alexandria against all avowed Christians. The elderly Deaconess Apollinia became a target of the blood-thirsty mob. They battered all her teeth out with stones then led her, covered in her blood, toothless, with a broken jaw, to a huge fire outside the city gates. The choice of renouncing her faith and offering prayers to the Roman Gods or being burnt alive, was offered to her. Apollinia asked for a moment to consider, her captors released their hold of her and she threw herself on to the fire. All this happened in the year AD249 and her martyrdom didn't go unnoticed by the Church, because she was canonised in AD300. A medallion of St Apollinia was issued in the 13th century which many believed would stop the wearer suffering from toothache. It was only a short step from there that St Apolline, as she was later called, became the Patron Saint of Dentists.

Chapel of St. Appoline

In 1054, William Richenoht, who owned all the land around Perelle Bay in Guernsey, decided to become a monk at the Monastery of Mont St Michel. He gave all his land and worldly goods to the Monastery in the hope that God would forgive him his many and great sins. The Abbey became the Seigneurie of the area although parcels of land were leased out to certain local farmers.

It was for one of these parcels of land that, in 1392, Nicholas Henry acquired a licence from the Abbey of Mont St Michel to build a small chantry chapel. These chapels were popular among the rich people of the time and were for their own private use. The chapel built by Nicholas Henry became one of 19 known private chantry chapels built in Guernsey during the 13th and 14th centuries. A charter of King Richard II, dated 20 March, 1394, granted the right of Nicholas Henry to build a dwelling place near the chapel, then known as La Chapelle de Saint Marie de la Perelle, a house for a chaplain whose sole duty would be to celebrate divine service every day for both Nicholas and his wife Philippe.

Later the chapel was known as La Chapelle de Notre Dame de la Perelle before being dedicated to St Apolline sometime before 1452 when an Act of the Royal Court of Guernsey on 6 June, 1452, mentions the chapel as La Chapelle Saint Appolyne.

The chapel has passed through the hands of many Guernsey families over the years. From the Henry family it passed to the Guille family and then the Seigneur of Anneville, Edmond de Chesney bought the land and chapel. Later, the Fouachin family acquired the land and then, by inheritance, the chapel became the property of the family of Andros. The small chapel ended up as part of the farm standing opposite the small parcel of land on which it was built. This farm was owned by Pierre Lenfestey who died in 1879 and was the last private owner of the chapel. No longer used as a place of worship, Pierre Lenfestey found the chapel an ideal place for a stable and store. Hence over the years the Chapel of St Apolline became derelict.

In 1873, Sir Edgar MacCulloch persuaded the States of Guernsey to purchase the chapel from Pierre Lenfestey for the sum of £120. This made the chapel the first official ancient monument in Guernsey.

The chapel continued to remain derelict until 1972 when an appeal was launched, due to the efforts of the Rector of St Saviour, the Rev. Frank Cooper. The Guernsey Council of Churches made the appeal for £15,000, although by the end of 1979, when the appeal closed, the sum required for the restoration was £24,000. Great assistance was received from the Hayward Foundation and donations came from all over the world. Not every gift came in the form of money. An unknown dentist in Krakow, Poland, sent a wooden carving of St Apolline, the gift arrived from Poland in a shoe box.

Work commenced on the restoration of the chapel in February, 1976, when the old thatched roof was removed and a new roof of Cotswold Stone was laid on top of the new timbers. The cost of the roof alone was £5,000 with the remainder of the money donated being spent on York stone paving flags, a Purbeck stone altar, new pews and stained glass windows.

The vaulted ceiling contains a late 14th century fresco showing the four evangelists with the Virgin Mary holding Jesus in her arms. During the period the chapel was used as a store, the fresco became faded and in parts, totally obscured. The internationally known artist, Mrs Eve Baker, was commissioned to restore the fresco to its former glory and lights have been placed on the wall to illuminate the work of art.

The small chantry chapel of St Apolline measures 27ft in length, 13ft 9 inches wide and has an area of 300 sq.ft. There are three small narrow square headed windows and two doors, one of which is only about 4ft high. The chapel also has a bell-cote which has been completely restored.

On 9 October, 1978, at 5p.m. a rededication ceremony took place. The Lord Bishop of Winchester and the Catholic Apostolic of Jersey were present as the chapel has now become a place of prayer for Christian unity.

Guernsey's oldest chapel joins only a few other places of worship to be dedicated to the memory of the Patron Saint of Dentists. Others can be found in Florence, Rome and in the Cathedral of Rouen. When the feast of St Apolline is celebrated on 9 February each year it can be certain that the smallest gathering will be inside the tiny chapel of St Apolline in St Saviour, Guernsey.

SPECIAL DELIVERY

ON MONDAY, 3rd July, 1905, the following notice appeared in the *"Evening Standard"*.

"Postmasters may arrange for the conduct of a person to an address by an express messenger".

Henry Turner was a man with a keen sense of humour plus a liking for the unusual. He was a well known public figure in his native island of Guernsey and in his short autobiography, described himself as the Sherlock Holmes of Guernsey, having no equal in running down to earth any absconding defaulters. He was one of the principal promoters of the public meeting which took place in Hyde Park to plead for the liberation of Dreyfus. Henry Turner had also caught the public's attention when he knelt on the steps of the Town Hall and raised the Clameur de Haro, although his reason for doing so has not been recorded.

On reading the notice in the *Evening Standard*, Henry Turner decided to put the Guernsey Post Office to the test. The following morning he presented himself at Smith Street Post Office and proclaimed that he wished to be posted to Jersey. The bewildered counter clerk had not read the *Evening Standard,* therefore thought he was the subject of a practical joke. Henry Turner produced a copy of the paper which caused further confusion. The clerk decided to pass this unusual customer on to the Postmaster, Mr. P. Marinel, who asked for the request to be put in writing. Mr. Turner replied that he would do so and proposed to return the following morning when he wished to be posted to Sark.

When Mr. Marinel opened for business the next day he was greeted by an immaculately dressed Henry Turner armed with his request in writing. Mr. Marinel informed Turner that to cover the boat crossing and safe delivery there would be a charge of 5s.10d. If desired, the messenger boy could also return the "Parcel" back to Guernsey for a further payment of 4s 5d. Turner agreed to the cost of the two way journey, handed over the amount, and the official forms were completed, although much to Turner's dismay, no stamp was required.

A young messenger boy, William Gunney, was assigned the unusual task of delivering the live "Parcel" and at 9.30a.m. the pair walked from Smith Street to the Albert Pier where they boarded the "Alert". At 10.00a.m. they set sail for Sark with messenger Gunney making certain he didn't mislay his "Parcel" by remaining a few feet from Henry Turner during the entire crossing. On arrival in Sark the "Parcel" was escorted up the hill and handed over to the Sub-Postmaster, Mr. F. Baker, who signed the form as proof the "Parcel" had been duly delivered. At 11.15a.m. Henry Turner sent the following telegram; "To Smith Street Postmaster. Express Messenger did his duty satisfactorily with courtesy. Worthy of being promoted Sergeant. Turner."

The first man to be posted to Sark

Due to the fact Turner had booked a return passage, Gunney continued to shadow his "Parcel". After a visit to the Rev. and Mrs. Seichan, the pair went for a drive by horse and carriage before partaking lunch at the Dixcart Hotel. Gunney then walked his charge back to the boat for the 5.00p.m. sailing which landed them in Guernsey one hour later. News of Henry Turner's latest escapade had brought hundreds of people down to the docks. Numerous friends shook his hand, congratulating him on his posting. Henry, now in a buoyant mood, took William Gunney for high tea at Mrs. Ward's cafe in Fountain Street. During the meal he promised Gunney a present for his services and, true to his word, the next morning gave the lad a pocket book and a framed photograph of the pair preparing to leave for Sark. Later Henry Turner published a set of photographs to commemorate his deed and these have become collectors items.

A postscript was published on Tuesday, 16th January, 1906, by the *Guernsey Star* in the form of the following poem.

"There shall not be posted, or conveyed, or delivered by Post, except with the special permission of the Postmaster-General, any living creature." July 1905.

This item by Sir H.T. was read;
In him the sense of humour's not dead;
So, thinks he, I'll test this;
Such a joke I could not miss;
But here's off to the P.O. he said.
So he arranged as a parcel he'd be;
Put in charge of a boy named G;
Then he paid five and ten;
Started off there and then;
On the "Alert" to brave wind and sea.
Although bound for the island of Sark;
Don't think it was only a lark;
An end he had in view;
His mind made up to pursue;
And to Guernsey return before dark.
Still in charge of Messenger Gunney;
Who dubbed the affair very funny;
Midst admiring gazes;
Tho' perspiring like blazes;
He wouldn't have missed it for money.

At the Post Office they duly arrive;
The time then about 11.05;
Here, not to be escheated;
The "Parcel" is receipted;
Sir Henry and the boy go for a drive.
The next move is to Dixcart Hotel;
Where the boy and his charge fare well;
Then feeling quite elate;
They depart in high state;
Leaving the Sarkese the great news to tell.
How Sir Henry as a "Parcel" was sent;
And what gave them lively content;
Was that which he had done;
Th' last dodge 'neath the sun;
Was of use, and not mere sentiment.

LES CASQUETTES

THE Channel Islands have many rocky outcrops around their shores which, over the centuries, have accounted for hundreds of unfortunate vessels. Storms and dense fog have caused ships through the ages, from Roman galleys to modern day oil tankers, to come to grief on these outposts of treacherous rocks. The island of Alderney is close to one of the most dangerous hazards to shipping around our shores, namely, Les Casquettes.

At the time of the Ice Age the English Channel was merely a great river which flowed to the north of Alderney, continuing out into the Atlantic Ocean. As the ice melted and water covered great expanses of land, this river slowly turned into the English Channel and the old river became the infamous Hurd Deep, where many ships have perished. The rocks of Les Casquettes are like great tentacles which reach out to collect the vessels after they have fallen foul of a storm in the Hurd Deep. The main shipping line from Dover passes close by therefore ensuring a constant supply of ships who on foggy nights, or whilst being lashed by a dreadful storm, founder on Les Casquettes.

In 1119 "The White Lady" was lost whilst transporting Prince William, only son of King Henry I, from France to England. It has always been supposed that the ship had fallen foul of Les Casquettes although it is now believed the vessel might have foundered on rocks close to the French coast.

In 1695 history recalls the tragic tale of the "Mary" and her unfortunate crew. Those who managed to clamber on to the rocks before their ship sunk faced a terrible nightmare; hunger. Their first act of self preservation was to eat the ship's dog. Later, by the drawing of lots, the survivors ate two members of the crew. When finally they were rescued only 10 out of 22 were alive and two of these died on their way to England.

Les Casquettes, sometimes called Casquets or Caskets, was owned by Thomas Le Cocq who received a visit by a large group of shipowners in 1722 asking for a light to be installed on the rocks. Thomas Le Cocq sent a request to the King who, with the blessing of Trinity House, granted a licence for the construction of a lighthouse. Work commenced immediately with the building of three towers; St Peter; St Thomas and Donjon; each about 30ft high and in the shape of a triangle. Three towers, built in this shape, made the lights of Les Casquettes totally different from any other lighthouse in Britain or France therefore easily recognisable by mariners. The light came from an armourer's forge, enclosed in a glazed lantern, which was kept alight by the use of bellows. The constant spray would have made this an extremely arduous task for the keepers who worked on a shift basis. The lights were first lit on the 30th October, 1724, and helped to keep many passing ships from a watery grave. Le Cocq held a 60 year lease on the lighthouse at an annual rental of £50. For providing a light on the Casquettes he was allowed to collect dues from all passing ships although in some cases this proved difficult.

Les Casquettes

In 1770, the armourer's forge was replaced by oil lamps thereby making the keepers job slightly easier. These lamps didn't help the H.M.S. Victory on the 4th October, 1744, when a great storm caught her in the vicinity of the Hurd Deep. The lighthouse keeper heard two shots and, although some wreckage was washed up later on the shores of Alderney, no trace was ever found of the crew of 1,100 men.

Trinity House took over the running of the light in 1785 and they installed the new Argand lamps which in 1818 were improved with revolving lights as a further aid to mariners. The keepers received regular supplies by boat from Alderney although they had transported some soil from the northern island to construct a small garden where they managed to grow a few vegetables to supplement their diet.

The original houses suffered storm damage in 1823 so new accommodation had to be built. It was soon after this that Lucas Houguez took over the task of lighthouse keeper. His term of office lasted for 18 years during which time neither he nor his family left the rocks. Finally he became paralysed due to the constant damp and retired to his home in Alderney with a life pension. Incredible tales are told about his family during their 18 year ordeal on Les Casquettes. A census, taken in 1841, gives the names and ages of the family, listing their place of abode as Casquettes. Lucas was 45 as was his wife Mary. Their six children were Mary aged 20, Peter 18, Elizabeth 12, Ann 10, Harriet and Simon 5. Life on the rock must have been hard for the keeper but for the young children, totally cut off from an outside world they had never seen, it must have been a strange existence. Visitors to the rock took presents of books and dolls and the children marvelled at a picture of a cow. An Alderney carpenter, sent to undertake some work on Les Casquettes, fell in love with Mary, the eldest daughter. She agreed to go to Alderney with him but found the bright lights of St Anne plus the general pace and noise of life in the big city too much for her, and so she returned to her family. Later when Lucas retired, the pair were re-united and married on Alderney. Swinburne brought the plight of this young girl to life in one of his great poems called "Les Casquettes".

In 1854, the tower of St Peter was increased to the height of 120 feet above sea level thereby giving a visibility of 17 miles. A small harbour had been constructed and the keeper would hoist a blue flag if conditions were safe to land or a white flag if unsafe. By 1877, only St Peter remained as the other two towers were demolished, one became a store whilst the other housed the foghorn. In 1952, electricity was introduced and later a helipad was built. This made transportation of staff and maintenance a great deal easier.

During the Second World War, Les Casquettes were abandoned. The light was closed down on 21st June, 1940, and the keepers taken, along with the inhabitants of Alderney, to the sister island of Guernsey.

The Germans took over the lighthouse and fortifications can still be found there today. Various commando raids were carried out against Les Casquettes by the British forces, including Operation Dryad on the 2/3 October, 1942. Captain John Lewis was given the task of leading the raid due to his knowledge of local waters. Seven Germans were taken prisoner and top secret code books were also obtained. On one raid the Germans were taken by total surprise and one soldier was found asleep complete with hair net. At the end of the war 30 Germans were removed from Les Casquettes by H.M.S. Lynx and taken to Guernsey.

As with most lighthouses of today, Les Casquettes has recently become fully automatic. Three quick flashes every 30 seconds warns seamen of the treacherous group of rocks whilst charts, plus modern equipment, have now reduced shipping losses to a minimum. The gulls are now the only inhabitants with just the occasional maintenance man for company. Although Les Casquettes is now a much safer place, a certain amount of the mystery and character of the rock has been lost with the passing of people such as Lucas Houguez and his family.

MILK-O-PUNCH SUNDAY

A GROUP of young men hurried across a field, bucket in hand, to where a lone cow was tethered. Eggs, taken from a neighbour's henhouse, were broken into the pail and mixed with sugar. The bucket was then placed under the cow. One young man, braver or more knowledgeable than his companions, started to milk the animal. Once the required amount of fresh, warm milk had been obtained, nutmeg was added to the mixture. A bottle of rum was produced from someone's coat pocket and slowly poured into the pail, while another member of the group stirred carefully, to stop any curdling. Mugs suddenly appeared in everyone's hand and the group of men helped themselves from the pail, to a liberal amount of Milk-o-Punch.

Milk-O-Punch Sunday at The Divers. Photograph: Ilona Soane-Sands

This tradition was re-enacted on the first Sunday in May on the island of Alderney. No one can remember when or how it started, as traditions are handed down through many generations, some remain, others are lost with the passing of time. Some of the locals of Alderney are reknowned for their liking of a tipple, therefore any custom which allows them to have a free drink, without reprimand from the farmers concerned, is all right with them and should be continued.

The first Sunday in May is traditionally the beginning of spring, when the cows are allowed out into the fields after the long winter indoors. On this day the cows were considered to be public property, therefore anyone could avail themselves of the milk. You had to provide your own rum and any extra ingredients you wished, to make the punch to your taste. The eggs and milk however, were free to anyone who wished to take them. The cows must have hated this custom as they were surely milked by many people who had never milked a cow before. The fresher the eggs and warmer the milk the better the punch would be.

Today, thankfully for both farmers and cows, the tradition has been taken over by the various publicans of the island. Every host supplies a free glass of Milk-o-Punch to each customer and every recipe varies slightly in its content. Some use cinnamon, others have secret ingredients which have been handed down from father to son. Many islanders sample the different recipes and compare like with like by visiting as many public houses as their legs can stand in the time provided for free drinks to be served. The large bowl standing on each bar soon empties as people stagger from bar to bar in an endeavour to find the best recipe of the year.

With so many customs and traditions dying out all over the world, due to what we call progress, it is pleasing to find an ancient custom which still prevails in our northern island. Well done Alderney, long may you continue the tradition of Milk-o-Punch Sunday.

THE MASTER OF SEMPILL

DURING the early 1930's one of the main topics of conversation throughout the world concerned flying. Airports were springing up in most countries and the Channel Islands were not left out of this new adventure. Jersey Airways were already operating from West Park beach and plans were in an advanced stage for airports to be built in the islands of Jersey, Guernsey and Alderney. To the layman, the smaller islands of Sark and Herm would have appeared unsuitable to be considered for aerodromes. There were certain people who had other ideas.

Sir William Francis Forbes-Sempill was born on the 24th of September, 1893. He became known as the Master of Sempill from birth until his father's death on the 28th February, 1934, when he graduated to the title of the 19th Lord Sempill. He had a distinguished career in the Royal Air Force during the First World War after which he held numerous high ranking appointments including leading a British Aviation Mission in 1921 to organize, equip and train the Imperial Japanese Naval Air Service.

The Master of Sempill was a great friend of the Dame of Sark and Sir Percival Perry, later Lord Perry, who had taken over the lease of Herm from Sir Compton MacKenzie in 1923. Lord Perry was the chairman of the Ford Motor Company in England as well as being involved in numerous other enterprises. He was a man of vision and always on the outlook for any interesting new business venture. The small island of Herm was his retreat and he disturbed not only the peace of his small domain but also a few of the older inhabitants when he introduced a Ford lorry onto the island. New fangled contraptions had no place on Herm so when it accidentally slipped into the harbour there were a few wry smiles from the locals. All efforts to extradite the vehicle failed and eventually it was covered in concrete to become a permanent part of the new jetty where Lord Perry was to anchor his yacht. Many other sources give 1933 as the date of the first Ford lorry on Herm. In fact this was when the replacement truck arrived which ended its days as a rusty heap on the common due to the lack of a good mechanic. Edward Searson worked on Herm from 1925 until 1927 then returned in 1930 until 1937. One of his many tasks was to drive the Ford truck and he well remembers the fate of the first vehicle. Mr Searson also remembers the Master of Sempill. The locals on Herm may have been unhappy about motorised transport on their small island but you can imagine their astonishment when the Master of Sempill landed his private aircraft on the common. A certain portion of the common had been turned into a golf course and it was here the small light aircraft touched down sometime in 1933. Edward Searson was sent with the Ford truck to deliver a large cannister of high grade aviation fuel to enable the Master of Sempill to refuel his aircraft. Lord Perry had adapted the machinery used for heating the

White House to use aviation fuel. A bull calf was also loaded, legs securely tied, onto the rear seat of the plane. The Master of Sempill then took off, circled around the island, passing low over the White House, his face clearly visible as he waved goodbye to Lord Perry and his guests.

This was the first visit by the Master of Sempill. A few months later he landed again on the common and it was during this visit that plans were formulated for constructing an airfield on Herm. In fact a few weeks after his visit, a large machine weighing over five tons, was brought ashore and taken to the common. The road grading machine was never used and plans of an airfield never materialized to disturb the local inhabitants of Herm.

The Master of Sempill was no stranger to the islands. In April, 1931, he became the first man to land an aircraft on Sark. His mission was to deliver Mr Beaumont, son of the Dame of Sark, home for his holidays. Sir William Sempill returned again in 1932, first with some unknown passengers, then again with the London newspapers. On the first Sunday in August, 1932, he collected a heifer, a present from the Dame of Sark. This was the first heifer ever shipped from the Channel Islands to the mainland by air. The Dame of Sark also played host to two Cambridge undergraduates in 1935 when they landed in a field adjoining her property.

During this period Jersey Airways were contemplating an airfield on Sark. A farm property known as "La Genetiere" was sold to a Guernsey resident on condition he leased one of the fields to Jersey Airways. Farmers on Sark were horrified and united in their opposition to the idea of an airfield, saying the noise would frighten their cattle.

Whether it was local opposition or the high cost of building an airfield is uncertain. Nevertheless plans were shelved and the residents of Sark and Herm have never been bothered by anything noisier than a few tractors. Lord Perry left the island of Herm at the beginning of the Second World War and the Master of Sempill never again disturbed the airspace of these peaceful havens.

A SECOND POSTING

HENRY Turner may have been the first Channel Islander to post himself from Guernsey to another island, but his feat was most certainly not unique. Whether Major L. Palmer had read of Turner's exploits is unknown, nevertheless, on Wednesday, 21st February, 1940, another live parcel was mailed out of Guernsey, this time bound for Alderney.

With war clouds looming on the horizon, travel between the islands was becoming increasingly difficult. Even though the regular steamers continued to ply the waters, they offered restricted seating for the ordinary passenger, because space was taken up by military personnel. Major Palmer had concluded his business and wanted to return to Alderney to rejoin his wife in the family home. The Sark Motor Ships Ltd, who operated the service between Guernsey and Alderney, could only accommodate twelve passengers, and most of these seats were occupied by the military. On Friday, 16th February, Major Palmer attempted to book his passage home without success. The following Monday he tried again, only to be informed the Wednesday sailing was already fully booked.

By this time, he had installed himself comfortably in the Royal Hotel, and although every amenity was readily available, his main wish was to be transported to the waiting arms of his wife in Alderney. He therefore presented himself to the Guernsey Post Office and requested to be mailed home. The Postmaster decided this unusual request would require the consent of the Head Post Office in London. After consulting with his superiors, it was discovered the laws contained in the Post Office Guide did in fact allow humans, on condition they were accompanied by a courier, to be transported as "Mail". The appropriate fee was 6d per mile.

Therefore on Wednesday, 21st February, 1940, at 8.30 a.m. Mr. Jock Clark, a G.P.O. Postman, left his home in New Road, St. Sampson's, and travelled to the Royal Hotel where he collected Major Palmer and transported him to the docks where "Joybelle III" was preparing to sail for Alderney. A label had been attached to Major Palmer's buttonhole with the following instructions; "On His Majesty's Service. Official Paid, Harbour Master. Alderney."

Captain Ingrouille of the Joybelle was uncertain whether he should accept the package, because he already had a full passenger list. Fortunately two people did not claim their seats therefore Major Palmer and his courier were permitted to board the vessel. However the Captain charged the normal fare for passengers, making Major Palmer's home journey extremely expensive. The 20 mile trip passed without further incident and the Palmer family were re-united in Alderney.

The "Posting" was reported in the local papers which brought forward a postscript on Friday 23rd, under Letters to the Editor. An anonymous person, who signed himself Veritas, brought to the public's attention an interesting footnote. The Sark Motor Ships Ltd, were under contract to transport His Majesty's mail between the islands and could not refuse to carry any form of mail, even if it turned out to be male. Another fact uncovered by Veritas concerned the Captain's responsibility in case of an accident. If the ship had sunk, he would first have to see to the safety of his passengers and only then, if possible, save the mail.

As yet no person has ever tried to emulate the adventures of Henry Turner and Major Palmer, thereby saving the Post Office the problem of transporting further human mail between the islands.

LA GRAN'MÈRE DU CIMÉTIÈRE

THERE has been a village in St. Martin's for hundreds of years. A map of Guernsey, drawn up in the early 18th century, shows approximately 26 houses surrounding the old Parish Church. People have worshipped on the site of the church since man first inhabited the earth. A Neolithic tomb occupied the site and Pagan meetings were held around the old stone structure. St. Martin has inherited a souvenir from those far off days in the form of the Statue-Menhir known as La Gran'Mère du Cimétière.

There are many of these monuments throughout Europe, and Guernsey boasts two fine examples. One found in the grounds of Câtel Church, which dates back to 2,500BC is much less artistic than La Gran'Mère. The old lady in St. Martin was almost certainly carved much later, although it is impossible to fix an exact date. Some historians claim she was made around the same time as the Goddess of Câtel, whilst another train of thought puts her carving as late as 600BC.

It is thought the head of La Gran'Mère was remodelled during Gallo-Roman times, when better tools could have been brought to bear on the granite block. This would account for the clearly defined features as opposed to the many other Statue-Menhirs. At the time of her construction, La Gran'Mère would have represented a Goddess, probably of fertility and curer of ills. People paid homage to the old lady, and the custom of placing flowers and coins on her head and around the statue, still remains today. Many weddings which take place at St. Martin, finish with the Bride and Groom posing for pictures beside La Gran'Mère. Flowers from the wedding bouquet plus an offering of money will nearly always be left with the Goddess in the hope that she will give the happy couple a long healthy life together and bless their union with children.

La Gran'Mère has occupied different positions in the churchyard throughout the ages. Truly living up to the old saying, "Shunted around from pillar to post."

A Mr. Carey tried to buy the Menhir for his rose garden although his daughter persuaded the Rector of St. Martin to keep La Gran'Mère within the bounds of church property by using the old lady as a gatepost.

In 1860, a certain Churchwarden, unimpressed by history, felt La Gran'Mère should be destroyed, as a Pagan Goddess had no place on the consecrated ground of a Christian Church. He had the statue broken in half, which aroused such indignation amongst the parishoners that they had it repaired by fixing metal rods into the two pieces of granite so that La Gran'Mère was restored to her former glory.

During 1932, the *Guernsey Press* was inundated with letters to the editor from outraged readers. They wanted La Gran'Mère moved back into the safety of the churchyard. The general feeling of concern was that a heavy vehicle might go out of control and damage, or even worse, destroy, the Menhir. They also objected to the ancient Goddess being part of a gatepost. The Churchwardens were against finding a suitable position inside the confines of the cemetery, although La Gran'Mère was rescued from the task of holding up the gate.

Today La Gran'Mère du Cimétière stands on silent guard at one of the entrances to St. Martin's Church. How many wedding photographs have featured the Goddess will never be known, neither do we know whether her supposed powers still work, thereby giving the happy couple a long healthy life and a marriage blessed with an abundance of offspring.

La Gran' Mère du Cimétière

EMPIRE ELECTRIC THEATRE

IN the early part of the 20th century St. Sampson's was a thriving port, therefore numerous amenities sprung up around the area to cater for the requirements of the locals. One such amenity was the Empire Electric Theatre.

Situated in the old Salvation Army Hall, which is now the premises of La Bonne Vie, the theatre, which was also known as the Empire Palace, opened its doors on Monday, 16th September, 1912. The actual picture house was upstairs with the door for public use on the side of the building. Under the management of Mr. J. E. Smith, the theatre set out to provide the public with the finest up-to-date subject films. The advert in the Guernsey Evening Press which announced the opening night listed the films to be shown as follows;

Love Finds A Way	A Grand Vitagraph Drama.
Hypnotic Detective	Drama.
The Local Bully	Cowboy.
Foolshead's Innocence	An Amusing Comedy.
Man From The Foothills	A Very Fine Drama.
The Right Remedy	Pathe Comic.
Billy Bungle Burglar	An Amusing Comedy.
Blind Heroine	Drama.
Jewels	Edison Drama.
Trial Of Tales	A Roaring Comic.

Doors were to open at 7.30 p.m. with the films commencing at 8.00 p.m. sharp. Admission costs were 3d for a cushion seat and 6d for chairs. There was also to be a children's matinee on Saturday afternoons when the charge was 1d. Especially for clients from St. Peter Port there were late cars which left St Sampson for town at the end of the performance every Monday and Thursday.

The opening night was reported as being a great success with a full house thoroughly enjoying the entertainment provided. Mr. Buttberg accompanied the films on the piano and during rousing scenes the audience would stamp their feet in time with his music. He became well known for his constant shouting of "Keep your feet quiet."

Another pianist to appear at the theatre was Doris Carroll who would go to the theatre during the morning to watch the various films on offer. She would then be able to decide which music would suit the different moods of the pictures beforehand.

Local acts would also be hired to perform between the various films whilst the reels were being changed. One such act was Yarmouth Brown and his three sons. They were a vocal act who specialised in audience participation. The sons would march around the stage encouraging the crowd to join in with their father and clap in time with the song.

The list of films were changed regularly and many people booked a permanent seat in the theatre on a certain night of the week.

The theatre continued to flourish until a final list of films were displayed for viewing on Saturday 7th March, 1914. For this programme the audience were to be treated to the following array;

Special re-engagement of the Three Chips - Featuring new songs and dances.

Portia . . . . Great Detective Drama In Five Parts.
The New Curate. . . . . Comedy.
Transit Of Venus . . . . Comedy.
Island Of New Zanbia. . . . . Travel
The Moonlight Trail . . . . Drama.
Uncle's Last Will . . . . Comedy.

On Monday 9th March, 1914, an advert appeared in the *Guernsey Evening Press* informing all clients that the Empire Electric Theatre was closed until further notice for re-decorating and repairs.

This advert remained in the paper each night until Wednesday 18th March, when it was changed to; "The Empire Theatre. Watch this space for the opening night. St. Sampson's."

On Tuesday 14th April, the size of this nightly advert was reduced by half and the public were kept waiting for news of the opening night until Wednesday 13th May, 1914, when the advert appeared for the last time. After that date no further information was given to the public and without any trace the Empire Electric Theatre disappeared from the skyline of St. Sampson's forever.

THE PICQUET HOUSE

SINCE the early 1700's there had been a military guard house situated on the South Esplanade. Prisoners were kept in custody in this building when rough weather prevented them from being transported to the jail which was at Castle Cornet.

In 1818 the British Government decided they wished to construct a more permanent guard house near the site. This request met with strong opposition. On Wednesday 25th November, 1818, Col. John Guille, Commander of the North Light Infantry Regiment of Guernsey Militia made a speech to the States. He criticized the States for even considering to allow such a construction saying that he was against the British being allowed to have any official building in the island and if a guard house was to be built then it should be placed in the hands of the Militia.

The Lt. Governor at the time was Major-General Bayly who was not popular with the local inhabitants. He accused John Guille of not mustering the Militia quickly or efficiently enough for parade duties and ordered his dismissal on the 30th of November. Many States members and locals realised that the true reason for replacing John Guille was his speech to the States and therefore the Commander of the Militia received a great deal of support. John Guille wrote back to the Lt. Governor saying he had no authority to dismiss anyone in the Militia. He also wrote to Whitehall informing them of the situation but to no avail. His dismissal stood and the British Government had their way.

The Picquet House was therefore constructed on the South Esplanade for the use of the British troops primarily as a detention area for soldiers who misbehaved. They were also on hand if there was any trouble in St. Peter Port and a deterent against unwelcome visitors who landed at the harbour.

The architect was a Mr. Goodwin, and the total cost of building the guard house and quay in front amounted to £648 18s 10d. Guernsey granite was used by the builders and the construction had a 65ft frontage on the South Esplanade and 48ft in Church Street. It consisted of a guard room, 22ft by 25ft; living quarters which measured 15ft 6 inches by 22ft; plus a detention room 18ft by 10ft. Each of these rooms were 13ft high. There was also a toilet; coal store; plus one other store. Two small yards were provided for exercise and the building had electric light and running water.

It must have been a long night whilst on duty at the guard house, even when the soldiers had time to relax, as only plank beds had been provided. The Picquet House was probably not the favourite place for the British troops stationed in Guernsey.

For almost one hundred years the Picquet House continued to be used by the troops until in the early 1900's, it was deserted and became derelict,

The Picquet House

which caused the British Government to decide to sell the property. An auction took place on Wednesday 21st July, 1926, when a large crowd gathered at the Picquet House to watch the auctioneer from A. Martin & Son, whose office was at 6, Court Row, St. Peter Port, attempt to obtain the best possible price for the landmark. There was a slight delay in the advertised starting time of 2.00 p.m. in order to allow the crowd to gather within hearing distance. At 2.15 p.m. the auction was opened with a bid of £700. Bids rose at £50 a time until the hammer fell when bidding stopped at £1,650. The successful bid had been placed by Mr. G. F. Peek on behalf of the Guernsey Bus Company. The auction had been conducted on behalf of the Officer Commanding the Royal Engineers (Guernsey & Alderney District) who requested that 10% of the purchase price should be deposited with the auctioneer by 1.00 p.m. the following day. The remainder was to be settled on passing contract which had to be no later than one month after the date of auction. In all, the auction had lasted only 13 minutes and the Picquet House now belonged to Guernsey just as John Guille had maintained it should have from the beginning.

Numerous offices now have taken space in the building which has changed hands on a few occasions. On the 30th July, 1981, it was last sold by Steiner Investments Ltd of Manor Place, St. Peter Port, to Trafalgar Travel Holdings Ltd, 1, The Queen's Road, St. Peter Port, who sometime in 1984/5 changed their name to Picquet Holdings Ltd.

John Guille wasn't in favour of the building in 1818 and it is doubtful if he would be in favour today of the Picquet House which is covered with posters. The only sign of the original purpose of the building is the large granite stone which remains on the frontage, this reads; "Erected by Government AD 1819 Major-General Bayly Lt-Governor".

ALDERNEY WINS MURATTI

THIS was the unusual headline featured in the evening papers of all the Channel Islands on Friday, 30th April, 1920. The small northern island had triumphed against all odds to beat her larger rivals for the Muratti Vase.

The Muratti, Cup Final of Channel Islands football, began in 1905 with a Guernsey victory. The triangular competition, one semi-final, and a grand final, was not held during the five years of the First World War, but it recommenced in 1920 after hostilities with the Germans had come to an end. The year 1920 saw Jersey take on Guernsey in the semi-final at the Cycling Ground in Guernsey. Thursday, 15th April, proved to be a damp day, not only for the spectators who watched the match, but for the Jersey side when they were bundled out of the competition by one goal to nil. Guernsey now had to play Alderney in the final, and most betting men put their money on Guernsey.

The final was due to take place at Westmount in Jersey although an attempt was made to switch the match to Guernsey, to enable the spectators from both competing islands to have easier access to see the game. Alderney however, did not agree with the switch. They felt that any Jersey support would be firmly in their favour, as no Jerseyman would shout for a Guernsey team, and besides, they didn't want to give Guernsey the home advantage.

Therefore on Thursday, 29th April, at 3.30 p.m. the teams kicked off at Westmount for what was to be a memorable final. The sun shone, although a strong wind blew across the pitch, as over 4,500 people gathered to watch the minnows take on the whale. Admission for the game was 6d, while a seat in the pavilion was 1s.6d. The referee was Mr. R. Pook from Portsmouth and the sides lined-up as follows;

Alderney. Jennings; McLernon;(Capt) Catts; Allen; Olliver; Gadie; Hammond; Baker; Lihou; Attwell; Pike.

Guernsey. Aubert; Curtis; Le Cheminant; Brown;(Capt) McAvoy; S.Chapple; Keyho; H.Chapple; Warr; Rich; Blicq.

The game was fast and furious, with chances at both ends. The Alderney goalkeeper, who played a magnificent match, saved the ball from entering the net on many occasions with a series of unbelievable saves that had the Jersey fans applauding for all they were worth. Alderney had been right to stage the game at Westmount. The local supporters shouted their approval every time one of the Alderney players touched the ball. Midway through the first half, Alderney's Pike was brought down and had to be carried off the pitch with an ankle injury, after which he took no further part in the game.

As if the task of beating Guernsey had not been great enough, Alderney were then down to ten men (it was to be many years before substitutes were allowed in football matches). It now seemed inevitable that Guernsey would

From back row to front row includes:
*A.Machin, B. Anquitell, W. Mclernon, Bob Mclernon,
W. Parmentier, B. Newton, A. Henson, N.Griyer,
W. Hammond, Sam Allen, T. Oliver, J. Gadie, T. Le Cocq,
Alfie Allen, T. Smith, S. Newton, Jack Hammond,
T. Baker, Bonnie Newton, ? Bideau.
Photo courtesy of Alderney Society and Museum*

make sure of the game with at least one goal before half-time. Jennings brought off save after save, and the frustration started to show in the Guernsey play. Then the miracle happened. A few minutes before half-time Lihou was put clear with only the goalkeeper to beat. His low shot went underneath the body of the Guernsey keeper and Alderney were in front.

The second half saw Guernsey throw all their expertise at the Alderney goal. Jennings played far above himself and the ball seemed to stick to his hands from every cross or shot. Even the famous Irish International, Pat Jennings, would have been proud of the display of goalkeeping shown by his namesake. Time slowly ticked by, with the local crowd looking at their watches as the last agonising minutes crept by. After what seemed an eternity, the referee finally blew his whistle and Alderney had the Muratti Vase for the first time.

Amid scenes of wild jubilation, the trophy was presented to the winning captain by Sir Alexander Wilson, Lieut-Governor of Jersey. Laps of honour had not yet become part of football, but if any team ever deserved one, the

Alderney team should have been the first to observe this now familiar ritual in English finals.

Alderney have never since been able to lift the trophy high, although they always show great courage and determination when playing their opponents in the semi-finals. In 1921, when they attempted to defend the trophy, they faced Jersey and took the home side to extra time, before going down by two goals to nil. Jersey then went on to beat Guernsey in the final, by the only goal.

Many years have passed since that epic day at Westmount in 1920 and Alderney still await their second victory. There must be many people in all of the islands, while wishing to see their own team do well, would love to see the small northern island repeat their 1920 performance and once again take the Muratti Vase back to Alderney.

FIRST BRITISH POST BOXES

THE idea of providing permanent boxes at convenient positions through- out a city, enabling people to post their letters, dates back to 1653. These first post boxes appeared in Paris though were not received with much enthusiasm by the Parisians. After a short trial period the boxes were removed although they were re-introduced in 1758. Gradually the scheme gained public support and by 1829, post boxes could be found throughout most regions of France.

Anthony Trollope, later to become the famous novelist, worked as a Post Office surveyor who district included the Channel Islands. During a visit to France he had inspected their post boxes and felt the system could work in Britain. As a small area of Britain would be required to test public opinion, Trollope paid an official visit to Jersey from 4th to 12th November, 1851, then to Guernsey to ascertain whether the islands would be suitable for his requirements. On his return to Exeter on the 30th, he wrote to his immediate superior, Mr. Creswell, chief surveyor of the Western District of England, and put forward his proposition concerning the installation of post boxes in the Channel Islands. The scheme was passed on to the Postmaster General, Lord Clanricarde, who sanctioned the experiment.

On 23rd November, 1852, the first post boxes in Britain became operational in Jersey. These were situated in David Place, New Street, Cheapside and St. Clement's Road. They proved extremely popular and on the 8th February, 1853, the inhabitants of Guernsey were also able to make use of post boxes. Number 1 was situated at 12, Union Street, number 2 at 5, Hauteville and number 3 at The Piette.

All the post boxes used in the Channel Islands were cast in Jersey at the works of Messers Le Feuvre in Bath Street. The blacksmith who undertook the work was John Baudains (some sources give his name as John Vaudin) with the cost of each box amounting to £7.00. The boxes were emptied each morning, except Sunday, in time for any mail destined for the mainland to be despatched to London the same day.

The experiment proved successful and after two years the Post Office introduced boxes throughout London, after which little red boxes could be found the length and breadth of Britain.

Over the years all the original post boxes in the Channel Islands, except the number 1 box at 12, Union Street in Guernsey, were either replaced or transferred to postal museums. In October, 1980, the Post Office changed their image by painting all their boxes deep blue. Guernsey's number 1 box was situated in the grounds of a hotel. When the Post Office workers arrived, armed with paint and brushes, the owner of the hotel stopped them from applying blue paint to the oldest box in the land. He contacted certain States members and over the next few years, numerous debates and letters

First British Post Box

concerning the colour of this one particular post box filled the pages of the *Guernsey Press*.

In September, 1987, the workers returned to Union Street, only this time their paint pot contained the original maroon paint.

At 3.00 p.m. on 7th October, 1987, a short ceremony took place in Union Street. Mr. Derick Ray, Chairman of the British Philatelic Federation Congress, unveiled a plaque which had been attached to the railings in front of the post box. The inscription on the plaque read as follows,

"The British Post Office installed its earliest roadside posting boxes in the Channel Islands in 1852/3; this box is the oldest survivor still in daily use in the British Isles. It has been restored to what is believed to be the original livery of that era."

The post box had stood on the spot for 134 years although the life of the plaque was a great deal shorter. Within the space of one month it was sadly reported in the *Guernsey Press* that vandals had removed the commemorative plaque from the railings.

The number one post box is still in use today and one can only wonder as to just how many letters and cards have been "Popped in the Post" during its many years of service.

THE LITTLE CHAPEL

ONE of Guernsey's many tourist attractions can be found at Les Vauxbelets where, situated in the beautiful valley just below the estate owned by the De La Salle Brothers, stands the Little Chapel of Brother Déodat.

The order of the Brothers of De La Salle arrived in Guernsey on the 20th of June 1904 after a law had been passed in France banning all types of religious schools. The Brothers of the Christian Schools was started in Paris in 1680 by Jean-Baptiste de la Salle. He came from a wealthy family of the city of Reims where he was christened on the 30th April 1651. The De La Salle schools and colleges found in most parts of the world go back to the efforts of Jean-Baptiste and his many followers.

Brother Déodat, who arrived in Guernsey on the 5th of December, 1913, was just one of hundreds of Brothers who had come to help educate the youngsters of the small Channel Island. He fell in love with the peaceful valley at Les Vauxbelets and decided to build a Grotto similar to the famous landmark at Lourdes. He began this monumental task during March, 1914, and quickly built a small chapel, 9ft long by 4½ ft wide. Due to some criticism of the size and a few unkind jokes about his work, he spent one evening of the early summer pulling down the chapel.

However he did not give up, and by July, 1914, he had finished a Grotto which was officially blessed on the day of the outbreak of the First World War.

After its completion he built a second chapel just 9ft long by 6ft wide, which could hold only four people. In 1923 the Right Reverend Cotter, Bishop of Portsmouth, visited the island and being a large man, he couldn't enter through the door of the chapel in order to hold mass, so in September of that year, Brother Déodat once again brought his handiwork to the ground.

The Little Chapel which stands at Les Vauxbelets today was started soon afterwards and the shell of the building took two years to complete. Brother Déodat decided to decorate the walls of his chapel using pieces of broken china, shells and pebbles. He spent hours foraging around for broken china and started the long laborious task of covering the walls. Help came from the Daily Mirror in the form of an article, complete with photographs, published in 1925, on the efforts of the De La Salle Brother to build and decorate the Little Chapel. The following Sunday hundreds of islanders made their way to Les Vauxbelets armed with boxes of broken china. Gifts of china came in from all over the world and one particularly beautiful piece of mother of pearl depicting St George defeating the dragon was sent from the Lieut-Governor of Guernsey.

The interior of the main chapel is 18 feet long by 10 feet wide with a beautifully ornamented domed roof. A statue of the Virgin Mary gazes down upon the altar and crucifix, which has been decorated to a great extent, with ormer shells.

The Little Chapel

Two smaller crypts can be found at the end of a small staircase; the Chapel of Perpetual Succour and the Crypt of Passion. Brother Déodat's copy of the Grotto of Lourdes is outside the Little Chapel alongside a rockpool, complete with a mosaic map of the city of Lourdes. Watching over the rock-pool is a magnificent replica of the Cross of Calvary.

A mass of colour greets all who come to visit this remarkable work of art. The intricate patterns of shells, china and mother of pearl gives only a small insight of the years of Brother Déodat's painstaking labour of love, which has formed this unique monument to his faith in God.

His task completed, Brother Déodat, who was in ill health, left the island in 1939 just before the Second World War began, to return to France. He died on the 21st November, 1951, aged 73.

The maintenance of the chapel was entrusted to Brother Cephas until his retirement in 1965. After which the upkeep was taken over by a special committee formed in 1977 who have renovated both the roof and foundations to make certain the Little Chapel of Brother Déodat will remain as an attraction to the thousands of tourists who will visit Guernsey for many years to come.

VICTORIA TOWER

MONDAY, 24th August, 1846, was a day of great celebration in Guernsey. Queen Victoria, accompanied by the Prince Consort, became the first British Monarch to set foot in the island. Many islanders felt there should be some permanent reminder of this auspicious occasion. Consequently a committee was formed who put forward the idea of constructing a tower in honour of the Royal Visit. A subscription list was started and on Wednesday, 9th December, 1846, the committee met at the Assembly Rooms under the Chairmanship of Sir William Collings. The meeting was informed a total of £1,060 had been donated, with the amount from each parish as follows; St. Peter Port £900; St. Martin £57; St. Sampson £15; Vale £28; Câtel £60. A further donation of land had been received from the heirs of the estate of Peter Mourant, who had owned the site of the New Ground Mill. This site had originally housed a menhir known as La Pierre L'Hyvreuse. The most recent building had been L'Hyvreuse Mill which had been demolished by the previous owner. The committee decided to proceed with the construction of the tower which would be known as Victoria Tower.

The foundation stone was laid on Queen Victoria's birthday, May 27th, 1848. A grand fete was organized to celebrate the occasion, with the entire town of St. Peter Port decked in flags and floral tributes. Flags were also flown at Castle Cornet and Fort George, home of the Island Militia, and arches had been constructed over the road at Vauvert and at the entrance to the site of the tower. Many people, eager to obtain a good view of the official ceremony, had gathered near the tower before 9.00 a.m. One hour earlier, members of the Loyalty and Mariner's Lodges of Freemasons had congregated in the Assembly Rooms. Once they were attired in their masonic regalia, and after a short private ceremony, they joined the procession at 9.30 a.m. which was headed by the band of the 1st Regiment of Militia, plus a guard of the 16th Depot. The entourage marched through the streets lined with thousands of cheering people, until reaching the site of the tower.

The Lieut-Governor, Major General J. Bell, arrived at 10.00 a.m. and was presented with a masonic apron and a silver trowel. After arranging the mortar he struck the stone three times with an ivory mallet and declared the foundation stone of the tower to be well and truly laid.

The Lieut-Governor also completed two further ceremonies that morning. Into a small niche in the wall of the tower he placed a glass vase which contained a Sovereign, half Sovereign, an English crown, half a crown, a shilling, sixpence, two silver fourpenny pieces, an English penny and halfpenny, plus a Guernsey penny, halfpenny and double. Accompanying the coins in the vase was a brass plaque, 7½ inches square, on which had been engraved the following inscription,

Victoria Tower

"The foundation stone of this tower, erected to commemorate the visit to this Island of Her Most Gracious Majesty Queen Victoria and of her Royal Consort, Prince Albert, on the 24th of August, 1846, was laid on the 27th May, 1848, by His Excellency Major-General John Bell, C.B. Lieut-Governor."

There also followed a list of the names of members of the committee which can also be found engraved in stone just inside the door of the tower. This stone reads,

"This Tower was built by Public Subscription aided by the States. Committee. Thomas Carey Esq; Sir William Collings; John Valrent Esq; Commissary Gen Tupper Carey; Frederick-Corbin Lukis; Robert MacCulloch; Edgar MacCulloch."

The architect for the tower was William B. Collings of London and the surveyor, Richard P.D. Goodwin. The building contract was placed in the hands of a local firm, Matthieu and Jacques Tostevin, and the final cost of construction amounted to £2,000. The stone used for the tower, which was 100ft high, was red granite, taken from the quarries at Cobo.

At the completion of the first two ceremonies, Lady Bell named the Tower and everyone bowed their heads in a prayer of dedication. The Militia Artillery fired a 21 gun salute which was followed by the playing of the National Anthem.

Lieut-Governor Bell then proceeded to present new Colours to the four regiments of the Militia who were parading on the New Ground. This was followed by a further gun salute from both the Militia and the 16th Depot at Fort George.

The festivities continued well into the evening and it appeared every inhabitant of Guernsey was determined to celebrate the Queen's birthday and commemoration of her visit in grand style.

Just outside Victoria Tower, in the grounds of the well maintained gardens, can be found two cannons. These guns were presented to the Island of Guernsey by Her Majesty's Government in 1856 as a trophy of the Russian War. On 20th October, 1857, the States ordered carriages to be cast, which would enable them to mount the cannon for display. The Woolwich Arsenal carried out this assignment at a cost of £16 each carriage. The two 24 pounders, complete with carriages, arrived on May 21st, 1858, and add the finishing touch to the gandeur of Victoria Tower.

SILVER MINES ON SARK

OVER the generations Sark has received her fair share of invaders. There was St Magloire and his 62 monks in AD 568 who founded a Monastery on the island. Eustace the Monk, in 1212 tried to capture all the Channel Islands, but only managed to take Sark until Philippe d'Aubigny, warden of the islands, defeated Eustace in 1214, thereby regaining control of the small island. In 1338, Admiral Béhuchet of France captured all the islands except Jersey and again on 21st July, 1549, the French took control of Sark. Fortunately they were defeated when they attempted to take Guernsey and Sark was left deserted until the arrival of Helier de Carteret.

From his home in St Ouen, Sark was clearly visible to Helier de Carteret and knowing the island was unpopulated, he set sail and landed there in September, 1563. He received a charter from Queen Elizabeth granting him the rights to the island on condition that he maintained 40 men on the island to hold it safe for the Queen. He therefore became the first Seigneur of Sark. One section of the charter granted the Seigneur all the mining rights which later brought another invasion of Sark; this time by Cornish miners.

From as early as 1609 there had been rumours of mineral deposits on Sark although nothing was ever done until 1833 when John Hunt arrived from Chiselborough in England. He was a mining engineer and, on investigating the area around Creux à Pôt, he found a vein of copper and silver. The de Carterets had been Seigneurs from 1565 until 1720 when they sold their rights. Peter Le Pelley was now the Seigneur and therefore held all the mining rights on the island. John Hunt received a concession from Le Pelley to open mine shafts and the contract was signed on the 17th October, 1834. Hunt had to pay £1 annual rental as well as give Le Pelley 6% of all the ore brought to the surface, the lease was to run for 31 years, but was later amended to 39 years.

Work commenced at the end of 1834 with 250 Cornish miners being brought over to open the shafts. Their efforts were confined to Little Sark around the eastern coast known as Le Pôt. Over 70 locals were also employed and for a few years more people dwelt on Little Sark than lived on the whole island at any time during its history. No great quantity of ore was discovered and a further dramatic setback occurred on 1st March, 1839, when Peter Le Pelley was drowned in a boating accident off Pointe du Nez.

His brother Ernest became Seigneur and showed great interest in mining. He mortgaged his Seigneur's Rights for £4,000 to help the cost of more mining equipment. A man out shooting climbed down the cliffs at Port Gorey to retrieve a rabbit when he discovered some rocks containing a strong silver content. This was the start of the most productive of the four mines known as Sark's Hope. This shaft went to a depth of 360 feet with one gallery

LITTLE SARK. — Ruins of Silver Mines.
Les Ruines des Mines. — LL.

Silver Mines on Sark

extending 300 feet out under the sea bed. The Le Pelley shaft had a depth of 600 feet, Prince shaft 366 feet and Engine shaft 480 feet.

John Hunt also tried mining in Guernsey, Herm and Brecqhou and had formed the Guernsey and Sark Mining Company, whose offices were at 25 Commercial Arcade in St Peter Port. Two hundred shares of £5 each were issued with Hunt holding 30 and Le Pelley 10. With more money constantly needed, Hunt placed a silver tea and coffee set made of Sark silver in the office window to attract investors.

A landing place had been blasted at Port Gorey and a narrow gauge railway was used to bring equipment to the mines and carry the ore to the waiting boats.

Good quality ore could fetch up to £600 per ton, but all the shafts were drying up and the company was getting further into debt. The final nail in the coffin was the flooding by sea water of Sark's Hope. This had been the most productive shaft and no further capital remained to purchase pumps to empty the flooded galleries. The total cost of the mining operation had been £34,000 with the yield only 25,000 ounces of silver, plus several tons of lead which fetched £4,000. The machinery was sold late in 1844 and all work ceased in 1845. Le Pelley tried to raise the money to pay back the mortgage on his Seigneur's Rights but finally sold out to Marie Collings in 1852.

This ended all mining in Sark. The Cornishmen went off to new mines being opened in America. John Hunt was left a broken man and Le Pelley had lost the Rights for his family to continue as Seigneur of Sark. As with past generations, the invaders retreated and left Sark in peace with only a few broken-down buildings, a couple of chimneys and some dangerous shafts as a reminder of the Guernsey and Sark Mining Company.

BUNGALOW HOTEL

THE Channel Islands are well known for their long association with tourism. Sark, although small by comparison with Jersey and Guernsey, boasts an excellent tourist trade. Most visitors stay on the main island of Sark although on Little Sark, the establishment known as La Sablonnerie, which dates back to the 16th century and was originally a farmhouse, entices many holidaymakers to return to the peace and tranquillity of the island. Today La Sablonnerie is the only major hotel on Little Sark although before the Second World War there was another hostelry open for tourists on this small peninsula of rock, called the Bungalow Hotel.

Nicholas Hamon, illegitimate son of shopkeeper Mary Hamon, was born on Sark in 1884. Sometime during 1913 Nicholas layed the foundations of a large building on Little Sark. Rumour has it he also found a quantity of timber which had been washed up by the tide. Whether or not there is any truth in this, Nicholas chose timber as the main construction material for his hotel. Only the chimneys of the 10 bedroomed hostelry were made of brick. Some of the bedrooms opened straight onto the patio, as did the large double doors of the dining room. Other facilities of the hotel included a library and an upstairs lounge with comfortable armchairs. Surrounding the lounge was a balcony where guests could enjoy the best views of the surrounding area. Nicholas also provided staff quarters and dug a well, originally operated by a wooden handle, for the hotel's water supply. All the lighting was by oil lamps and an abundance of flowers, which cascaded from the hanging baskets, decorated the establishment.

The first mention of the Bungalow Hotel can be found in the *Press Directory* of 1915. This is a simple listing of all property throughout the Bailiwick along with the tenants.

Further information comes from a publication called *Guide Book of Sark* by G & L Latrobe. Published in 1914 by Tozers of 10, Smith Street, St Peter Port, and costing 1/6. Here the Bungalow Hotel is listed as the fourth and newest hotel on Sark with a unique view from its commanding position and is extremely well placed for bathing.

Ward Lock & Co provide even greater detail in their *Illustrated Guide Book of the Channel Islands 1926*. The relevant passage reads as follows,

"Bungalow Hotel : Situated in a most beautiful position, stands about 345 feet above sea level, and is the only hotel with a magnificent uninterrupted sea view of Guernsey, Jersey, adjacent islands and coast of France. Spacious balcony and dining rooms with these views at the disposal of day visitors. Five minutes walk beyond the Coupee and near to Venus Bath, Black and White Caves, Port Gorey, Soufleur, Silver Mines, Pôt Bay, etc, with lovely walks to all parts of interest."

Bungalow Hotel

The guide book goes on to inform the reader about the noted Bungalow Home Made Cakes served for afternoon tea plus the speciality of chicken and lobster lunches. The hotel was fully licensed and provided transport to meet all boats to collect visitors and their luggage. Terms were moderate and bookings could be made by either telephoning Sark 5 or sending a telegram to Bungalow Hotel, Sark.

Numerous other advertisements indicate that the Bungalow Hotel also had its own Poultry Farm. In fact this side of the business must have been fairly large for Sark with 200 laying birds plus a further 200 baby chicks. Each egg had to be stamped by hand before being sold in the local store or to the other larger establishments on the island. Stocks, Bel Air and Dixcart each took 50 guests whilst the Bungalow Hotel could only provide accommodation for 20 paying customers.

In fact it was the Poultry Farm which started Nicholas Hamon's downfall. His wife Alice ran off with the man who helped with the daily running of the farm leaving Nicholas to manage both farm and hotel. This proved to be too great a task and eventually Nicholas found himself in financial difficulties and, in order to cover his debts, was forced to sell the lease of the Bungalow Hotel to George and Agnes Sharp.

George and Agnes had originally lived on the island of Alderney where George worked in the quarry. Due to a blasting accident he lost an eye which forced him to retire from quarrying. The couple moved to the island of Brecqhou where part of their employment was to row over to Sark for fresh water. With his black eye patch, a legacy from the accident, George must have resembled a modern day pirate as he approached Sark in his rowing boat.

George and Agnes Sharp took over the lease from Nicholas Hamon sometime during 1930 as the *Press Dictionary* of 1931 lists Nicholas Hamon at La Vauroque Farm and George Sharp at the Bungalow Hotel.

In his book *Sark as I found it* by Captain Ernest Platt, the writer describes the hotel as "Made for Lovers". In fact it was known as the Honeymooners Hotel, with Mr & Mrs Sharp in charge and sympathetic to newly married couples.

A few years later Nicholas Hamon met an untimely end. At 4.30 a.m. on the 9th December 1935, at Ivy Gates, Beauregard, he died of Cerebral Apoplexy, aged 51.

George and Agnes Sharp continued to serve their customers on the delightful balcony overlooking the other islands until the coming of the Germans. The Occupation not only meant the end of tourism but also the end of the Bungalow Hotel. Little Sark was heavily defended by the Germans with many of their men staying in the hotel. Later during 1942/43 the wooden hotel was taken down and used to enlarge the barracks on Little Sark. Material from many other bungalows was used for this work and over 200 marines were housed in the finished barracks.

On the 13th February, 1943, George and Agnes Sharp were deported to Germany. George was sent to Ilag VII, Laufen, OBB. whilst Agnes was sent to Compiegne. Later in early 1944 Agnes was transferred to Biberach where she was joined by her husband. In the Rolls supplied by the Red Cross dated 5th May, 1945, George, aged 65, had been given the internee number of 1010 whilst Agnes, aged 61, had the number 10056. At the end of the war both were returned safely to Sark were they lived out the remainder of their days. George died on the 8th May, 1962, in his 82nd year and Agnes on the 9th May, 1963, in her 79th year. Their grave can still be found in the small cemetery on Sark.

The Bungalow Hotel was never rebuilt and after the Occupation the wood taken to construct the barracks was sold off in various lots. A small bungalow has since been built on the original site and parts of the foundations and the patio are the only reminder of the old Bungalow Hotel which stood opposite Cider Press Cottage.

SIR PETER OSBORNE AND CASTLE CORNET

THE Channel Islands conflict with France began when King John lost control of Normandy in 1204 and the islands decided to remain faithful to the English Crown. The nearby coast of France, clearly visible on a fine day, then suddenly became enemy territory. Naturally the French wished to recapture the islands, therefore fortifications sprung up around the coastlines of each of the Channel Islands. The first records of Castle Cornet in Guernsey was in 1206, when building started on the stronghold situated on a rocky outcrop close to the entrance to St Peter Port harbour. There was no causeway in those days so the castle was totally cut off from the island. Castle Cornet controlled the sea route to the capital of Guernsey although, by being an island, it was also impregnable against assault from Guernsey.

At the commencement of the Hundred Years War the French did capture all the islands with the exception of Gorey Castle. In 1338, Admiral Béhuchet took control of Castle Cornet and the French enlarged much of the fortification, especially the area known as the Barbican.

Guernsey's original town jail was situated in Castle Cornet just as Jersey used Gorey Castle. During medieval times, prisoners sentenced to death were placed in a cage which was hung from the ramparts of the Barbican. They remained there, in full view of the town, until starvation and exposure brought about their inevitable death.

In both islands it was the custom for the Governor to live in the castle. In 1600, the Governor of Jersey, Sir Walter Raleigh, changed his abode from Gorey to Elizabeth Castle whilst his counterpart in Guernsey remained in Castle Cornet until 1672 when the gunpowder store blew up, killing seven people including the Governor's wife.

Sir Peter Osborne, born 1584, died 1652, became Governor of Guernsey in 1621 and would probably have had a quiet, peaceful and enjoyable existence whilst head of this lovely island had it not been for the Civil War in England. King Charles I had billeted 1,200 English troops in the island and they had run up the considerable bill of £4,650. Added to this was the ransom for two fishing boats who were captured by Algerian pirates whilst on their way back from Newfoundland. The King refused to pay both bills and therefore the sum had to be found by means of local taxes. When in 1643, Parliament issued an order for all Governors to be arrested, neither island complied, which resulted in the Bailiffs being deposed and the dissolution of the Royal Courts.

The people of Guernsey turned against the King, and Sir Peter Osborne, who was a staunch Royalist, retired with his troops to Castle Cornet. George de Carteret came from Jersey to visit Sir Peter and the Jurats sent the Sheriff to arrest de Carteret. Sir Peter Osborne refused the Sheriff entry into the

Castle Cornet

castle and de Carteret sailed back to Jersey. The following day the seige of Castle Cornet commenced. Lady Osborne was sent to live in St Malo for her own safety and on the 11th March, 1643, Sir Peter Osborne commenced shelling St Peter Port.

George de Carteret sent supplies to Castle Cornet from Jersey and even contemplated leading a force to recapture Guernsey for the Crown. Osborne informed him a Jersey attack would be strongly opposed in Guernsey and whilst his help with supplies was welcome, if not essential, it would be best to leave Guernsey alone.

Sir Peter Osborne continued shelling the town, usually on a Sunday morning when everyone would be going to church. During 1643 and 1644, some 30,000 cannon-balls were fired from the castle at St Peter Port. The constant barrage was maintained because the younger population of the town would roll the cannon-balls down to the harbour then row out to the castle and proceed to sell them back to Sir Peter for re-use. Without this unusual enterprise by the local youngsters, it is doubtful whether as much damage would have been done to the sea front properties as was otherwise sustained.

Sir Peter Osborne finally departed to join his wife in St Malo in 1646 when his place was taken by Sir Baldwin Wake. Castle Cornet continued to be held under seige through his reign as Governor until he finally disappeared under mysterious circumstances sometime late in 1649. Around the same time, Sir Peter Osborne, tired of life in exile, made his peace with Cromwell and returned to England from St Malo. George de Carteret hoped he would be made Governor of both islands but Lord Percy was appointed to take over at Castle Cornet. With the help of his second in command, Colonel Burgess, the garrison held out until the 19th December, 1651, when they finally surrendered. This was four days after de Carteret had marched out of Elizabeth Castle and handed over the island of Jersey to the Roundheads under the command of Colonel James Hearne. Both de Carteret and Burgess were allowed to travel, with their soldiers, to France and the Civil War was over as far as the Channel Islands were concerned.

Sir Peter Osborne died the following year back in his native England and peace was restored to the streets of St Peter Port and St Helier. Worshippers were able to go to church on Sunday mornings without the threat of cannon-balls falling in their midst, and the youngsters had to find new ways of earning a few extra shillings.

BEAUCETTE MARINA

ALTHOUGH the States of Guernsey have provided a large number of berths, for both local and visiting yachtsmen at the land reclamation site, the most picturesque anchorage can still be found at Beaucette Yacht Marina.

For many years until 1968 Beaucette Quarry had remained undisturbed. A derelict plot of waste ground, used for illegal dumping and a home only for rabbits, it was fast becoming an eyesore. A company called Vale Investments Ltd acquired the quarry and surrounding land and subsequently proceeded to obtain the necessary permission to change the landscape and use of the plot, into a Marina.

Beaucette Marina

In a *Billet D'Etat* dated Wednesday 26th June, 1968, the States Board of Administration lodged the following paper in the States. After consideration of the Report dated the 29th May 1968 of the States Board of Administration.

1. To direct the preparation of legislation by way of a Projet de Loi to control the development and use of Beaucette Quarry as a Yacht Marina, along the lines of the provisions set out in paragraph 11 of that Report and such incidental and supplementary provisions as may be necessary or expedient.

2. To authorise the President of the States Board of Administration, on behalf of the States, to enter into an Agreement with Vale Investments Ltd along the lines set out in paragragh 12 of that Report on condition that the Company consents to a Bond in favour of the States in the sum of £25,000 and charged on the premises of the Company to secure the payment to the States by the Company of any expenses which may be incurred by the States by reason of the failure of the Company to perform any of its obligations under the said Agreement, such Agreement and Bond to have effect until the coming into force of such legislation as aforesaid.

Final permission was granted on Friday 5th July 1968 and two days later a group of Royal Engineers landed at L'Ancresse from the ship "Sir Percival". Under the supervision of Captain Roger Jordan, Captain Graham Jarvis and Lieutenant Peter Page, the engineers and their vast array of equipment was brought ashore by pontoons.

The Royal Engineers had been assigned the task of blasting through the greenish granite, known as "Diorite" to allow the sea to flood the quarry on express orders of the Government who considered the project as valuable training for the men. During their stay the men were stationed in the Tomato Marketing Board's Hostel at Bulwer Avenue. It was thought the entire operation would last only a few weeks. Unfortunately the Guernsey granite wasn't to be moved as easily as anticipated and it wasn't until the morning of Thursday 10th October 1968, that the final blasting took place. Even though 12ft of tide covered the explosives, water was thrown over 30ft into the air. The entrance was now 55ft wide and 12ft deep at half tide, which allowed easy access into the marina at all states of the tide.

The Royal Engineers left the island on Monday 14th October although they returned on the 18th February 1969 aboard the *Agheile*. From their base at St Sampson's they transported their equipment comprising of compressors, generators, mechanical shovels and bulldozers by landing craft to the marina. The group of engineers, numbering 50 in all, blasted a further 5,500 tons of rock from the sea bed to make the floor of the marina level. Throughout this task they were constantly hampered by high winds and bad weather which caused rough seas to pound through the entrance of the marina.

Aerial View of Beaucette Marina

During the entire operation the engineers had used 2,450 lbs of plastic explosives, 630 primers and 41,500 ft of detonating cord. Over 15,000 tons of rock had been blasted and moved from the quarry. The total cost in man hours was estimated at £27,000 plus materials at £6,000. Questions regarding the expense to the British taxpayers concerning this costly exercise were asked in the House of Commons.

The only privately owned marina in the Channel Islands opened in June 1969. The site covers eight acres, half being the marina, the remainder taken up with a restaurant, offices and parking. The marina can hold 250 vessels, most of which berth on a permanent basis, although approximately 1,000 boats per year make use of the facilities for short stopovers. The surrounding land is 30ft above sea level which therefore offers complete shelter to the tallest of yachts. Although the entrance is 55ft wide, great care has to be taken when approaching the marina, especially from visiting yachtsmen who may not be familiar with the surrounding waters. The approach is from the Little Russel, halfway between Platte Fougere and Roustel Bns, approximately two cables south of Fort Doyle.

The ownership of Beaucette Marina has changed hands on numerous occasions. The original owners, Vale Investments Ltd, later changed their trading name to Channel Islands Yacht Marina Ltd. The company was wound up in 1975 when the marina was purchased by Mr Edward Fattorini under the name of Beaucette Marina (Guernsey) Ltd. Ownership of the marina changed again in 1982 when the company was bought by a consortium consisting of Richard John Anderson Brown, Mark Richard Anderson Brown, Sean James Anderson Brown, Shirley Wylie and Delia Lynn Clark. They continued to operate Beaucette until instructing Lovell & Partners to place the marina on the market in November 1985. Eventually Beaucette Marina was taken over by Roger Smith sometime in 1987.

One of the many changes made by Roger Smith was the purchase of the Spurnhead Lightship. The vessel, which had been built in 1959, at a cost of £98,843, was 114ft long and weighed 242 tons. It arrived in Guernsey on Saturday 20th February 1988 and was positioned to help visiting yachtsmen locate the entrance to the marina.

Although a larger and more modern marina has since been constructed in St Peter Port, the charm and comparative quiet of Beaucette, with its excellent restaurant and facilities, still draws yachtsmen towards the Little Russel and the entrance which took the Royal Engineers so long to blast from solid Guernsey granite.

ST. GEORGE'S HALL

ROLLER skating has been a popular pastime in Guernsey for over 100 years. Mr Wilfred Shirvell, a past owner of the Channel Islands Hotel, provided a maple floor especially for skaters during the late 1890's and early 1900's. The sport proved so popular that larger premises were required to cater for the growing number of people wishing to participate. Mr. P. E. Robilliard, who owned Piette Saw Mills, saw the potential in creating a new venue. He decided to turn part of his property into a large community hall, with special facilities for roller skating.

Work commenced in 1909 with the building quickly beginning to take shape. The small entrance on the Glategny Esplanade opened into a long corridor, ending in a vast hall, able to hold over 2,500 people. The total area covered 11,000 feet, with the hall rising to a height of 44 feet. The entire interior was painted pale green, and along with all the usual amenities, offered a main rink for skaters, 123ft by 43ft, plus the benefit of a learners rink measuring 52ft by 18ft.

In preparation for the opening, a sailmaker, Mr Hunkin, was employed to manufacture over 400 flags to decorate the hall. The skaters required music, therefore an orchestra was engaged to perform during both afternoon and evening sessions.

The grand opening was Christmas Eve, 1909, and the number of people who took advantage of the new facility slowly grew during the afternoon until the floor was totally crowded during the evening session.

For 4½ years St George's Hall continued to cater for skaters until the commencement of hostilities against the Germans. During August, 1914, the complex was taken over by Martin Brothers, the High Street tobacconists, who exported thousands of packets of cigarettes to the soldiers on the front line.

After the war ended, the hall was handed back to the skaters, although occasional dances and other functions were also held there.

One of the most memorable events to be staged at St George's Hall took place on Monday, 11th July, 1921, with the visit of King George V and Queen Mary. A notice appeared in the *Star* on Saturday, 9th July, under the heading "What Gentlemen Should Wear."

"It is suggested that gentlemen attending St George's Hall on Monday morning, should wear frock coats or dark suits, with gloves and ties of quiet colour."

Hundreds of suitably attired gentlemen, accompanied by their ladies all decked in their finest outfits, filled the hall to capacity. The public had been informed that certain members of island dignitary were to be honoured by the King during the event at St George's, although when it was announced that the Bailiff, Edward Chepmell Ozanne, was to be Knighted, a great gasp of amazement and approval echoed round the hall. The Bailiff was a most popular man and to be thus honoured on home soil, and in view of the large gathering, was seen as an excellent diplomatic move on behalf of the Crown and States.

A further royal visit took place in 1935, when the Prince of Wales, later King Edward VIII, attended a reception at St George's Hall.

The Second World War saw the hall take on another function. During the first year of occupation, the Germans held their own dances there until the complex became a flour store. Once the *Vega* began bringing Red Cross parcels to the island, the hall was also utilized as a storage depot for the parcels. The Germans transported the precious cargo from the docks to St George's on their railway which passed outside the door.

After 1945, the public once again were permitted to skate and dance in the hall. Trade shows, animal and flower shows, roller hockey, the Eisteddfod and even a Pantomime on ice were organised.

Two further royal visits to Guernsey were celebrated with receptions held at St George's Hall. Queen Elizabeth in 1957, followed by Princess Margaret in 1959, were both entertained in the island's largest complex of its day.

During the 1960's, the hall vibrated to the sounds of top English groups including the Beatles and Rolling Stones. Support for these groups was supplied by local bands, and for these occasions, two extra stages were built to enable three groups to set up their vast array of amplification in different sections of the hall.

In an attempt to form a new image, the hall was re-christened. Although advertised as The New Theatre Ballroom, most locals still retained the name St George's Hall when discussing future dates and outings.

With the opening of nightclubs and other similar venues catering for the youngsters of Guernsey, the days of St George's Hall were numbered. Finally, on Monday, 31st October, 1966, a dance was held to mark the end of an era. Over 900 people witnessed the closing scenes, as local bands, including Humble Fred and My Generation, played the last rites of St George's Hall.

The shell of the hall, in a dilapidated condition, is now surrounded by a modern business complex which bears the name of St George's Place. The small frontage of the hall on the Esplanade still remains as a reminder to passing locals of the good old days, when St George's Hall echoed to the laughter of skaters and dancers and when a Bailiff of Guernsey knelt before the King to receive the highest accolade of the land.

THE CHANNEL ISLANDS' FIRST AIRPORT

JERSEY Airport was very much in the public eye when it celebrated its 50th anniversary. Royal visitors, Concorde, the Red Arrows, plus hundreds of private aircraft paraded before the interested crowds. But when the first airport in the Channel Islands became 50-years-old, in 1986, the event seemed to pass almost unnoticed in Jersey and Guernsey. The people of Alderney, however, celebrated the opening of Blaye Airport with the knowledge that others may do things on a larger scale, but the tiny, most northern isle has the distinction of being the first to have an operational airport in the Channel Islands.

Among the people who gathered at the airport for the celebrations was one person who had more memories of the early days of flying than any of the others present. Mrs Wilma Bragg was the first Airport Controller, ticket seller, baggage handler, aircraft loader and girl Friday. In fact she virtually ran Blaye Airport single-handed. At just 22 years of age she had been chosen by Jersey Airlines to become the first woman in charge of an airport in Britain.

On April 1st, 1935, Judge Meelish, accompanied by Jurats of the Alderney Court, turned the first sod before allowing the tractors to take over the task of levelling out the airstrip. It had been hoped to commence operations some time during August of that year, but delays occured and the date was gradually postponed until Friday, March 27th, 1936, when Jersey Airlines flew to Alderney with just two paying passengers. The first to purchase his ticket and land was Mr Gordon Rice from Jersey. Although this was the first commercial landing in Alderney, it wasn't the first actual landing. In September 1935 an inspector had arrived from Guernsey to check the runway.

Alderney Airport was the brainchild of Harold G. Benest, a Jerseyman who ran Bellingham Travel and Jersey Airlines. Together with Jurat Le Cocq of Alderney, they negotiated with 40 Alderney residents who owned small parcels of land around Blaye for the lease of what was mostly barren headland. Harold Benest also built the Grand Hotel in Alderney, thereby introducing tourism to the Island.

Wilma Le Cocq – she was not married until during the War – was the daughter of Jurat Le Cocq, and was offered the job of running the small airport. She received six weeks training in Jersey where the aircraft were still using West Park beach. She then set up home in the tiny shed provided as an airport building. Inside the shed her working area was a wooden bench balanced on top of two 50-gallon oil drums. There was no official opening ceremony, Wilma just got down to work without any cutting of ribbons or speeches. Aircraft arrived at 8.15 a.m. and 6.30 p.m. every Sunday, Monday, Wednesday and Friday, with a scheduled turnaround time of ten minutes. In

De Havilland Dragons lined up on Jersey's West Park beach.

between flights Wilma was kept busy running the small office in St Anne from where she sold tickets, typed letters and kept the books.

To help with some of the heavy work, Wilma enlisted the aid of a pensioner, Sam Allen. He would mow the grass and help carry the baggage to the aircraft in a wheelbarrow. Sam was also helped by the local taxi-driver, Sid Simon, to man the fire brigade at the airport. This consisted of an open car with three fire extinguishers on the back seat. The customs officer was a retired Lieutenant Commander who didn't check the baggage but scrutinised the passports of anyone who wasn't British. This was the entire staff of what was, and probably still is, one of the smallest commercial airports in Britain.

There were no phones on Alderney at the time, so all messages had to be sent by telegram. This would usually work satisfactorily, although some unscheduled aircraft sometimes landed at Blaye. The pilots would fly around the Island to attract Wilma's attention, and she would leave whatever she was doing and rush to the airport in the company car so they could land. On one particular Bank Holiday there was a carnival in St Anne, and Wilma was taking part on a float depicting Henry VIII and his wives. Wilma was dressed as Anne Boleyn when an aircraft circled the Island. She rushed to the airport and pushed the steps out to the aircraft. Alderney is sometimes accused of being behind the times, but an aircraft met by Anne Boleyn did startle the few passengers.

Weather reports also caused some problems. If the grass airstrip was hit by a sudden downpour of rain, Wilma and Sam would put on their wellington boots and go out to inspect the runway. On occasions it would be too late to send a telegram to stop the incoming aircraft, so Wilma would stand in the middle of the runway and wave a white towel at the pilot, who would then turn back.

Another part of her job would be to remove the grazing cows from the runway when an aircraft was due. Any passengers who arrived and needed the urgent use of a toilet had to be directed to the nearest gorse bushes because the airport didn't have the necessary facilities. Wilma would also go round every Christmas to pay rent to the 40 landowners on whose land the airport was built. Her employment as Airport Controller was indeed more interesting and varied than her previous job, which had been school teacher to 18 six-year-olds at the old school, which now houses the local museum.

All good things have to come to an end, and the German Occupation saw the end of Wilma's employment at Blaye Airport. Along with all other Islanders she was evacuated to England where she handed in the books at the London office of Jersey Airlines. The pilots and staff were all joining the Fleet Air Arm, and Wilma was persuaded to join them. She became a Wren and served along with many other Channel Islanders during the Second World War. She didn't return to Alderney until 1948, by which time her sister had taken over the responsibility of running Blaye Airport.

Aurigny have long since taken over Blaye Airport, and the Rapides have given way to Trislanders. The buildings have been modernised with hangars and toilets, and fire engines have replaced the old fire extinguishers. Even so, there is still a certain magic about landing at Alderney Airport, and I'm sure Wilma Bragg still looks to the sky every time she hears an aircraft circling the Island.

OCCUPATION STAMPS

SINCE the introduction of the postage stamp, the Channel Islands had, until the Second World War, relied upon Britain for its supply of stamps. The idea of producing local stamps had never been considered until the German Occupation made the authorities of both main Islands carry out a complete re-appraisal of the situation.

The English stamps of the period were a definitive issue of King George VI which first came out in 1937, and a recently arrived Postal Centenary Issue depicting both Queen Victoria and King George VI, which went on sale on May 6th, 1940. The fact that the Germans arrived just six weeks after the Centenary Issue meant that larger than normal stock was to be found in the Post Office.

With 10,000 letters being posted each week, the supply of these stamps was soon greatly reduced. Postage within the Island at the time cost 1d, and the depletion in stocks of this stamp caused the Acting-Postmaster, Mr H. C. Chapell, to enlist the aid of the Bailiff of Guernsey, Victor G. Carey, in producing the format for the first Guernsey stamps.

But before this idea could be finalised, the stock of stamps became exhausted. The Germans suggested bisecting the 2d stamp and approval was obtained from H.M. Post Office. The following notice appeared in both the *Evening Press* and *The Star* on December 24th, 1940.

"The Post Office advises that further supplies of 1d postage stamps are not at present available and that, until further notice, prepayment of penny postage (for printed papers, etc) can be effected by using one half of a 2d stamp, provided that division is made by cutting the stamp diagonally. It is emphasised that the bisection of stamps should be done carefully and that correspondence bearing half stamps not cut in the manner indicated will be liable to surcharge."

First day covers of the 2d bisect were not available until December 27th, due to the closure of the Post Office over the Christmas period. It is estimated that appproximately 120,000 of the Centenary Issue were bisected, along with 40,000 of the King George VI definitive issue. Also a few thousand 2d stamps of King George were bisected.

Many of the occupying forces were keen philatelists and, along with local collectors, placed a great demand on the Post Office. Guernsey's first postage stamps were issued on Tuesday February 18th, 1941, and the bisect stamp ceased to be legal on Saturday February 22nd, having had a life of only 58 days. The 2d orange stamp faded from use, although it was to become a collectors item in the years ahead.

Guernsey was the first Channel Island to issue its own stamps because Jersey had a larger stock of British stamps at the outset of the Occupation. Designed by E. W. Vaudin and printed by the Guernsey Press, the stamps depicted the coat of arms with the words "Guernsey Postage". The 1d scarlet stamp went on sale on February 18th, 1941, followed by the ½d green on April 7th of the same year. This was followed on April 12th, 1944, with the 2½d ultramarine stamp. Shortage of paper caused some stamps to be produced on French water-marked paper which, during the gumming process, turned blue. This was due to the presence of a certain amount of oil in the gum being used, and these stamps were so sought after by collectors that they quickly sold out. The ½d only lasted from March 11th until March 31st, 1942, while the 1d stamp came out on April 7th and was sold out by April 25th.

Numerous variations of shades can be found, and problems with the cutters caused differences with the perforations. During March and April of 1945, all stocks of stamps had been used up, and a meter franking machine was used until the liberation of Guernsey.

Jersey issued its first stamp on April 1st, 1941. This was the 1d scarlet with the bright green ½d stamp going on sale on January 29th, 1942. Both stamps were designed by Major N. V. L. Rybot and printed by the *Jersey Evening Post*. They were of similar design to the Guernsey stamps, and due to shortage of paper were, at times, unavailable. Meter franking was used during one of these periods from May until August 1942. All the stamps produced locally had no watermarks and were printed on white paper.

Following a suggestion by the Germans, the States asked Edmund Blampied, the famous painter, to design a set of 6 pictorial stamps. The result was a beautiful set of stamps with the ½d green showing an old Jersey farm, and 480,000 of these were printed. The 1d scarlet depicted Portelet Bay and 840,000 were issued. Both these stamps came on sale on June 1st, 1943. On June 8th, the 1½d brown with a drawing of Corbière Lighthouse, and a sketch of Elizabeth Castle on the 2d orange/yellow came on the market, and 360,000 of each of these stamps were issued. The 2½d blue of Mont Orgueil Castle and the 3d violet with the famous scene of the gathering of vraic followed on June 29th. 720,000 copies of the 2½d stamp and 360,000 of the 3d stamp were printed.

The French government undertook the task of producing this set of stamps with the engraved plates being made by Monsieur Henri Cortot. They were printed at the works of Postes, Telegraphs et Telephones in Paris and have always been immensely popular with collectors. The 1d and 2½d issues were also produced on newsprint.

Today, the Islands enjoy a large revenue from the sale of local stamps, with collectors from all over the world placing orders at the philatelic bureau.

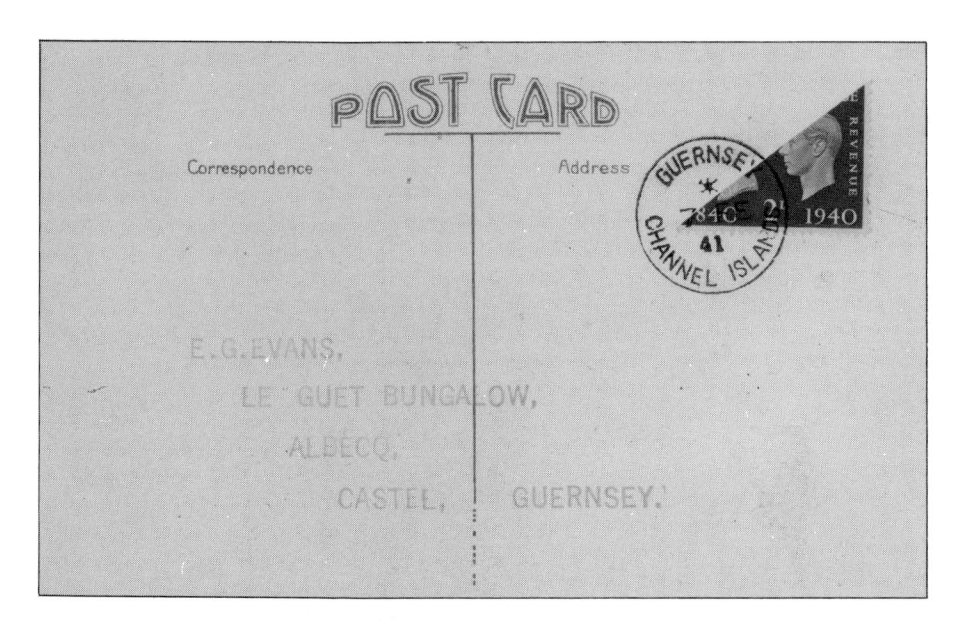

Many sets have come on the market since the Islands took over the local Post Offices, although none of the modern stamps hold as much value or memories as the stamps issued during the German Occupation.